Simple
Answers to
Your Questions
on the
Prophetic

Matthew Robert Payne

Please visit http://personal-prophecy-today.com to sow into Matthew's writing ministry, to request a personal prophecy or life coaching, or to contact him.

Cover designed by akira007 at fiverr.com.

Edited by Lisa Thompson at www.writebylisa.com You can email Lisa at writebylisa@gmail.com for your editing needs.

Paperback ISBN: 978-1-925845-08-2

DEDICATION

I dedicate this book to Jesus Christ, the prophet who mentored me for all these years. May this book bear great fruit.

A Note from My Editor

Dear Reader,

I love learning about prophetic gifts and about the office of the prophet. Since I have a prophetic anointing myself, this book especially interested me as I edited it for Matthew. The section about the twelve kinds of prophets fascinated me as God has created various types of prophets to minister to the Body of Christ. See if any of them resonate with you. And just wait until you read chapter 11! It's so powerful and encouraging.

If you are at all interested in the prophetic, this is a great book for you. It covers many relevant topics, including

- the difference between prophetic gifting and the office of a prophet
- dealing with struggles as a prophet
- finding your prophetic identity
- acceptance in your role as a prophet from your family and friends
- what to do when you feel like quitting
- and much more.

I appreciate the insights that Matthew shares from his wealth of life experiences of two decades as a prophet.

If you have any editing needs, I'm happy to help. Please see my website at
www.writebylisa.com or email me at writebylisa@gmail.com

Happy reading,

Lisa

TABLE OF CONTENTS

CHAPTER 1

How do I know if I'm called to be a prophet?

I guess there isn't a simple answer to that question. I have found that someone with a healthy interest in the prophetic is more likely to be called as a prophet. A lot of people enjoy the prophetic and enjoy receiving personal prophecies but not as many have committed to dedicating themselves to be a prophet. I guess you'd have to have a desire to be used prophetically to be called as a prophet. God places the prophetic calling on your life. He puts this burden on your heart to come forward and to be used in ministry by God.

From my early years when I was about twelve years old, I had a burden on my heart to be in full-time ministry. For most of my life, I thought that I would be an evangelist because I grew up in a Baptist church and only understood the role of pastor and evangelist. I didn't really understand the role of teacher, prophet, or apostle. I wasn't aware of what those roles did. One day, I heard an apostle teach on the five-fold ministry, and I found out about the calling of a prophet and that a prophet can be called to both Christians and non-Christians. I realized that that was probably my call, too, because by that time in my thirties, I felt called to the church.

One way of knowing if you're called as a prophet is to read prophetic books. If you have a healthy interest in the prophetic and in being a prophet, you'll devour books on the prophetic and read books that prophets have written about their calling and gifting.

The more that you find out about the role of a prophet, the more you come to realize that you have the DNA within yourself. One way to have a prophetic calling revealed to you is to hang around prophets, prophetic circles, and prophetic churches. Have prophetic people prophesy over you. If they say that you are called to be a prophet, this is one of the clearest signs for you. I read a book once by Bill Hamon, a famous prophet, about the prophetic, and he said 30 percent of the prophecies he gave were prophecies to people that were called as prophets.[1]

A large portion of the people he prophesied over were called to be prophets. That just shows me that people who are called to be prophetic or called to be prophets already have a healthy interest in the prophetic.

---

[1] Bill Hamon, PhD, *Prophets and Personal Prophecy: God's Prophetic Voice Today*, (Pennsylvania: Destiny Image, 1987).

That's why such a large percentage of the people he prophesied over were called to be prophets.

If someone prophesies over you that you are called to be a prophet, you can start to feel a little confidence that perhaps you do have a prophetic calling, and you won't lose or waste any of your time when you read books on the prophetic or by prophets. How do you feel when you read books by prophets? Do you feel a rush in your spirit, a rush of adrenaline? Do you relate to the stories? Do you resonate with what the prophets explain in these books?

I wrote a book called *Twenty-Two Signs that You're Called to Be a Prophet.* If you still have questions about whether you're called to be a prophet, I wrote that book for you. I encourage you to purchase it and read it and start to relieve your fears and stop wondering whether you're a prophet. Part of the office of a prophet, which takes many years to move into, is to call out the destiny in people, to call out their life purposes. As a prophet, you often prophesy to a person and tell them that they have a calling to be a prophet. Sometimes you're the first prophet who has ever prophesied their destiny over the person. As a prophet, you see more deeply than others, and you can gauge people's giftings and abilities.

To summarize, first of all, you have an interest in the prophetic. You'll want to read books about the prophetic. Second of all, prophetic people will prophesy over you that you are called to be a prophet. You might even have an established prophet prophesy this over you. Many people who are interested in the prophetic have prophetic giftings. They have the ability to prophesy, but that doesn't necessarily mean that they are called to be a prophet. But it certainly helps if you can receive the gift of prophecy and start to prophesy over people.

If you're a prophet, you'll start to feel the emotions of a prophet. You'll start to feel the mind of God and the heart of Jesus for people. You'll start to grow in your intimacy with Jesus and the Father, and you will draw closer to them. They'll speak to you more clearly.

The more you prophesy to people with the voice of God, the more likely that God's voice will become personal to you. He can inspire you and tell you through your intuition that you are called to be a prophet.

I recommend my book, *Twenty-Two Signs that You're Called to Be a Prophet*, for more information on this vital subject.

CHAPTER 2

Are all prophets the same?

I want to refer to a book written by James Goll, who I first found online. I watched his YouTube videos, and I was fortunate enough to hear him preach and meet him at the church I was attending. When he preached, he spent some time identifying twelve major types of prophet.

His message was very interesting. As I was listening, he had already covered nine types of prophets. I began to panic, thinking that I hadn't recognized any of the types of prophets that he had mentioned. I was sure that I was a prophet, but I did not recognize myself in any of what he said. Then he talked about number ten, prophetic equippers who teach the Body of Christ and who have a teaching gift.

I said to myself, "Well that's definitely me." I had written books, and I had it on my heart to teach and equip the Body of Christ. I'd run Facebook groups on equipping the Body of Christ through the prophetic.

I had already written books on the prophetic by then, so I knew I was a prophetic equipper. It really touched and blessed me.

Then he listed point number eleven, prophetic writers. I thought, *Praise God, I'm a writer*. I find much satisfaction in writing and producing books to equip the Body of Christ. I was definitely a writer and had written a few books by then, so I knew I was called to write for God. When he said prophetic writer, I said, "Praise God," again, and I recognized who I was.

Then he went on to point twelve, prophetic evangelists. Once again, at that time, I'd given more than ten thousand prophecies to strangers on the streets of my city, Sydney, Australia. I was definitely a prophetic evangelist. Out of the twelve prophetic types, I clearly identified as three of them.

As you read through the twelve different types of prophet, you will probably identify with one or more of these. You don't have to identify with each and every one of them. This information is taken from the book, *The Seer Expanded Edition, the Prophetic Power of Visions, Dreams and Open Heavens*.

James Goll says in that book, "The prophetic anointing of the Spirit makes itself known in a wide variety of ways. People are different, with different personalities, cultures, ethnic backgrounds, and gifts. As Rick Joyner often states, no two snowflakes are alike! It should not be surprising, then, that there is a greatly divergent expression of the ministry and office of the prophet. Although there surely are more, I want to look a little more closely at 12 variations of this prophetic grace. These various models represent what the Spirit is doing and desires to do in the Church. Together they present a more complete picture of the fullness of the Lord's prophetic anointing."[2]

I will list the twelve types of prophet. If you want a further explanation of what these prophets entail, I really encourage you to buy this book by James Goll, either as an e-book or in paperback.

1. Dreamers and visionaries, often called seers

2. Prophets who proclaim God's corporate purpose

3. Prophets who proclaim God's heart and standards for his people

4. Prophets who proclaim the churches' social responsibilities and actions

---

[2] James Goll, *The Seer Expanded Edition, the Prophetic Power of Visions, Dreams and Open Heavens*, (Pennsylvania: Destiny Image, 2012), p. 43.

5. Prophets who speak forth administrative strategies with a political slant (examples include Lance Wallnau and Praying Medic)

6. Prophetic worship leaders who usher in the manifest presence of God

7. Prophetic intercessors

8. Spirit bearers (please refer to James Goll's book for a more in-depth explanation)

9. Prophetic counselors

10. Prophetic equippers

11. Prophetic writers and

12. Prophetic evangelists.

I'd encourage you in your journey to keep exploring more about the prophetic, which is why you bought this book. I encourage you to spend your money and buy the book by James Goll and read these explanations of each of the twelve types of prophet. If you're called to be a prophet, you'll recognize which one you are. You'll recognize the function in which you are called. I pray that this chapter has blessed you and that you've learned something. I pray that it's whet your appetite to learn more.

I also want to encourage you to grow in your prophetic gifting by reading books, listening to teachings, watching YouTube videos, attending conferences, and sowing into prophetic ministries. You must continue to grow in your gifting. You can learn much from seasoned prophets, even though God will teach you as well. Becoming a mature prophet of God takes time and training and a teachable spirit. Never think that you have grown beyond learning from others.

CHAPTER 3

What is my function and role as a prophet?

As I've said, you can read James Goll's book to learn more about the types of prophets and what type of prophet that you're called to be. As a prophet, you are first called to be a friend of God. Your first function is as a close and dependable friend of Jesus. I don't believe that you can function as a respectable prophet who is honored without a close relationship with Jesus Christ.

Jesus Christ should become your closest friend. Jesus died for you and has given you every resource to become who you're destined to be. He's led you to this book and this resource to find out more about the prophetic. He has put it on my heart to produce yet another book on the prophetic. He clearly cares for you, so he led you to read this book.

What is your role? First of all, you are a friend of Jesus. You have to be a beloved friend of his. I wrote a book called *7 Keys to Intimacy with Jesus*. In it, I teach you how to develop a close, intimate relationship with Jesus.

Jesus said that one day, he will say, "Depart from me; I never knew you." (Paraphrased from Matthew 7:21–23.) Sadly, he will say that to some people who claim to be Christians in eternity, and they will be banished from heaven. One way to guarantee that Jesus won't say, "I never knew you," to you is for you to become his close and intimate friend.

Your main function as a prophet is to minister to the heart of Jesus. You can do that through prayer, worship, living out your destiny, and fulfilling your God-given purpose on earth.

First of all, your function is to be a friend of Jesus. Then Jesus wants to use you as his mouthpiece. He wants to speak to the people of earth and to the Christian church. He wants them to hear his voice.

In the current state of the church, many people can't hear Jesus speaking. Many people sit in churches, listening to dry sermons, dry religion, man's teachings, man's doctrines, and doctrines of demons, and they're not aware of the fresh, manifested voice of Jesus and the direction that Jesus wants the individuals in the church to travel. He needs representatives on earth—his ambassadors—to represent him, represent his words, and represent his desires on earth.

He wants you to speak to individuals and clearly explain their purpose and role on earth to them. He wants you to meet with and understand people and explain what their gifts and their talents are to them. He wants you to operate in churches and in the community and establish the purpose of the church, the community, the business, the organization, the political structure, or whatever he wants so that you can be a spokesman to bring God's design and perfect order to these places, buildings, and organizations of God's people.

God wants you to be set apart. He wants you to come out from your family and leave behind relationships, relationships that caused you to be unbalanced and relationships that caused you to lose your passion. He wants you to be filled with his passion and be his spokesman and his messenger to the people of the world.

What is your function as a prophet? What is your role? First, like I've covered, it is to be a friend of God, a friend of Jesus, and then to be his spokesman, to be someone who he can speak to, someone he can use to speak to the people of God, the individuals, that you run across and you do life with through your church and in the marketplace. He wants you to speak to structures in the church, in buildings, and in organizations.

He also wants you to speak in the marketplace and to businesses and corporations and bring his message and direction to those places.

It's a real honor and blessing to be used as the spokesman of God. It's a tremendous privilege to be chosen by God to speak on his behalf and to direct individuals and churches in his mission and his role.

Just recently, I was asked to give God's opinion about a conference at my church and to give them direction regarding conference organization. In the midst of the conference, my pastor asked me to speak a decree over the nation of Australia. I was officially recognized by my pastor as the prophet of the house. I hope that I have sufficiently answered your question here.

CHAPTER 4

Do other prophets become depressed?

One common characteristic among prophets and prophetic people is the calamity called depression. Prophets can be subject to a seasonal depression. They can come under the spell of clinical depression, and they might need to take medication to relieve the symptoms.

Of course, depression comes from the evil one. God doesn't give a prophet depression to teach him a lesson or to refine him. Depression is a work of the enemy, which can be very debilitating.

The answer to your question is yes, many prophets become depressed. In my own life, I have suffered with schizoaffective disorder, which is a combination of bipolar disorder and schizophrenia. I've had a bipolar condition, which is a combination of emotional highs and lows. For many years, I had seasonal depression and had to take medication to deal with it.

Sadly, the medication given by doctors used to make me high and manic, and it didn't work for me. I had to find a natural medication called St. John's wort, which used to relieve some of my symptoms of depression. I battled with depression for many years, until one day, through a ministry, I received deliverance. I've had some victory in not becoming as depressed as often as I used to.

You only have to look at the state of the world and the church and compare it with what God's best is and at his desires for the church and the world, and it will depress you. You only have to look at what is possible and what a Christian who's obeying Jesus and walking in the power of the Holy Spirit can do and see the shortcomings in the church, and you'll be depressed. You only have to experience some of that dimension yourself and walk in the prophetic and in miracles and signs and wonders to be saddened by most of what happens in churches.

This understanding of the wide gap between what is possible and what actually happens can be very depressing. The world can be a very depressing place. As a prophet, this can weigh heavily on you. You can have other factors that make you depressed. You can be rejected by people. You can feel as though you don't fit in. You might not have any real friends to interact with. Your life might be stripped apart, and you might be going through a refiner's fire. You can have all sorts of calamities, troubles, and trials in your life. These can cause you to become depressed and make you feel as if you want to give up and not go on.

In one Bible story, Jezebel threatened Elijah. Elijah ran off to a cave and felt like giving up his life and asked God to take his life from him. (See 1 Kings 19.) He was a powerful prophet who overcome the false prophets and caused a drought to happen in the nation of Israel. He had done some powerful, powerful signs, wonders, and miracles. He was a mighty prophet.

One word from Jezebel threatened his life, and he wanted to completely give up. He wanted to finish his life and go to heaven. If that's not a sign of depression, I don't know what it is.

We have other records of David weeping all night on his pillow. (See Psalm 6.) Jeremiah wished that he had never been born and cursed his mother for giving birth to him. (See Jeremiah 15:10.)

Many prophets in the Bible expressed their anxiety, depression, and struggles in their life. Depression was not foreign to David, Jeremiah, and to Elijah the prophet. I just used them as examples. Depression was not an unusual experience for these biblical prophets, and neither is it a strange thing for contemporary prophets.

The state of the church and this world is just depressing. If you focus too much on it, you can really go to a dark place, which is hard to cope with and live with. You have to understand your position; you have to understand why you're here. You have to release your message and hold your place and put these dark thoughts, musings, and wonderings aside into a special place in your heart so that they're not at the forefront of your mind. In this way, you won't be weighed down with depression.

If you find yourself dealing and struggling with depression, don't be surprised. Most prophets become depressed and go through bouts of depression for all their lives. It just seems to be a burden that prophets carry. It often leads them into living a more holy and a more separated life.

Depression isolates you from people because others don't really understand it. The burden that you bear as a prophet can be costly. I hope I've relieved your fears and answered your question.

CHAPTER 5

Do most prophets have to deal with rejection?

Like depression, rejection is a part of the prophetic calling. As a prophet, you're totally and radically different from the average Christian. You see life more deeply. You're more radically affected by the scriptures, worship, the holy commands of God, and what God wants and desires for people to do. The world and its environment seem to impact you. You have a high standard of holiness.

It affects you when you want to live a holy and righteous life, and you find that most Christians don't really care about that. You frequently receive revelations from God in the Bible. When you share those revelations with people, they look as though they are a deer caught in the headlights—shocked. They just don't understand what you're sharing. They don't understand your revelation. Rather than accepting the revelation as coming from God, they reject you. You can be very passionate and zealous as a prophet and always try to share revelation with your friends, but you are constantly rejected for what you know and what you have learned from the Holy Spirit.

It's serious. The average Christian isn't used to someone telling them how to live and how to change. These thoughts are constantly on your heart: sharing with people about a better way of living the Christian life. God is constantly speaking to you about how to live a better life and how to be consecrated and set apart to him. You want to share that with your friends or people you know at church.

They reject your words, your revelations, and your attitude. They reject you and think that you are holier or better than they are, that you think you're more knowledgeable than they are.

They tend to be jealous of you and of your walk with the Lord. You really wish that everyone could understand what you see in the Bible and that they could have a revelation of what you know and what you're experiencing with God. Yet the more you try and encourage your friends to see the message of the Bible through your lens with your eyes, the more they reject you. They might say that you're strange or that you're too zealous. They might say that you are single-minded and too passionate and that you've been brainwashed.

They might try and give you advice on who you should be listening to and what you should be doing. They sometimes try and cool you down, watering down your passion. They think you should be normal—whatever that is—and they encourage you to be healthy with variety and balance in your life.

These people care about you and try and change you and put out your fire. Yet nothing they say will have an effect on you. All you hear from their advice is rejection. When they want to change you, you take it as rejection. You feel rejection from people in church. You can start to question yourself about your calling and about why it is so difficult.

You ask yourself, *How am I going to be a prophet and affect people if I can't even impact my friends and the people at my church? How can I be used successfully and minister to people when the people who know me don't even listen to me?*

Jesus was wise when he said, "A prophet is not without honor, except in his own hometown and among his family." (Paraphrase of Mark 6:4.) I'm sure I will use that scripture again later in the book. It's so true that people can accept, respect, and even revere you outside your local church, but you can be rejected among your family, including at your own church. People reject you and think you're weird and strange. They want to bring you back into line and then give you advice on how to change your life. But it feels like rejection to you.

The key to this is not to be overtaken by a spirit of rejection, not to feel like a victim, or become identified with rejection.

I implore you to learn to forgive and forget and not live as a victim of rejection. Don't expect rejection but always be positive and outgoing and always keep your zeal and your passion for the Lord. You can hope that one day, the Lord will give you a friend to spend quality time with and discuss the deep things of God with and have a true and lasting friendship with.

You can pray for that kind of friend, someone to help you overcome your rejection. I have a friend, Nicola, who helps me with this.

Rejection can be used by God to thrust you into the arms of Jesus, to make you run to him and give you a fiery passion for him. But when you have a fiery passion for Jesus, you might suffer more rejection. I hope I've answered your question. Most prophets do deal with rejection. Rejection seems to be the main affliction that happens to prophets.

I dealt with rejection for many years and very few people understood me. But now I can say I am part of a church where I am accepted as a prophet and called to operate in my office and called for advice and instruction by my pastor. You need not be in the wilderness for all of your life.

CHAPTER 6

How can I find my voice as a prophet?

When people reject you and ask you to change and suggest ways in which you can change, you might be tempted to listen to them. You might be tempted to try and be someone different than who you are in order to stop the tide of rejection and make you more acceptable to others. Emerging prophets often try this; they try to conform to the Body of Christ and to the people in their church to make themselves more easily loved and accepted.

This is a mistake. Even though I am saying that it's a mistake, you might still try it. I will warn you just to be yourself and to express yourself as you see fit. But that won't stop you from trying to change as the pressure comes from your friends and family to be different and to change your ways.

Unfortunately, your friends and family have a lot of sway over you, and you're more emotionally invested in them than you are in an unknown prophet who's speaking to you from a book.

If you want to know how to find your voice as a prophet, my simple answer is to just be you. Post your thoughts and what you see and hear from God on Facebook. Be authentic, real, honest, and transparent. Don't be afraid to tell people your failures and trials and the troubles that you've been through.

People really relate to stories, and they especially come alive when someone shares a testimony. Jesus was a storyteller, and he went around telling stories, using stories in his parables, and really engaging with people. From my trips to heaven, I have seen Jesus interact with the children, and he shares stories from his childhood with them. Telling stories is a great idea.

As you express yourself, as you find your voice, make sure you're sharing stories about your life and about your experiences and about what you have figured out and what has been revealed to you.

Over time, with God's blessing, you'll find friends on Facebook or strangers that will come online and connect with you. They will start to encourage you and start to like and comment on your posts. Many of these strangers who sent you friend requests and who know your other friends will become the closest to you.

I have a friend on Facebook, Mary Gibson, who first learned about me by reading my books. At the end of all my books, I invite readers to become a Facebook friend. She became a Facebook friend and started to like and comment on my posts. I soon started to notice her comments. She liked me and loved what I was saying. One day, one of us reached out to the other. We started to call each other on Facebook Messenger. The relationship has really blossomed into a place where I count her as one of my dearest friends.

I am really encouraged by Mary as she has read all of my books and written reviews on them. Sometimes when writing a book, I think, *Well, what would Mary think? What would I say to her?* One way of finding your voice is by thinking about a friend, someone you know that you love. Speak directly to them. What would you say to them about the life of a prophet?

Mary's called to the prophetic and called to be a prophet. As I found these questions and answered them, spoke out my thoughts and wrote down these words, Mary was on my mind. One way to find your voice is to think of someone in your audience that you want to address and focus on them.

Focus on what you have to say to that person. How would you say it to them? How would you help that person with a unique life come to grips with what you're saying? You can put up a post on Facebook; you can start a blog and post to it. You can find your voice by posting on Facebook, or you can start to do YouTube videos. You can start to write books. You can wait for invitations to speak at your church. You can do many things without actually being invited to speak in church.

You can write articles. On one website, Ezine Articles, you can write articles for people to read. The site keeps track of how many people have read your articles each week.

You will become who you're meant to be. You will gradually find your voice and find that authentic you as you express yourself and are real. If some people on your Facebook page continually post critical comments and tear down what you say, I'd suggest that you unfriend or block those people. You don't ever want to be in a position of holding back and not saying what's on your heart on your own Facebook wall simply because of the pushback that certain friends will give you.

I'm very free and open and transparent with what I write and what I post. I post what's on my heart. I don't post what I think people want to hear.

I'm not affected by what I feel people will think about what I post. I post what's on my heart to post and as the Holy Spirit leads me. I write on subjects that the Holy Spirit leads me to write about. I don't worry about being careful with my words. When I write books, I don't worry about bad reviews that people might write. I don't let those thoughts enter how I find my voice.

CHAPTER 7

Why don't my church and family recognize me as a prophet?

Mark 6:4 says, "But Jesus said to them, "'A prophet is not without honor except in his own country, among his own relatives, and in his own house.'"

We know from scripture that when Jesus came to Nazareth, he found that he could do very few miracles. (See Mark 6:5.) This was mostly because the people of Nazareth knew him as a carpenter and as Joseph and Mary's son. They didn't know him as a miracle worker or as the Messiah. They didn't have the faith to believe that he was anyone special. They just knew him as a man who grew up in their community just like any normal man. They didn't have the respect or the honor that they should have shown the Son of God. Because of that, he couldn't perform miracles because they didn't have faith for him to perform miracles.

Can you imagine Jesus, who raised people from the dead, not having an effect on people? He walked on water. He turned water into wine. He healed blind people and lepers. And that miracle-working Jesus was held back from actually doing anything in his own hometown. Can you imagine that? What sort of unbelief would prevent him from operating as a miracle-working man since he was the Son of God?

It was simply because they supposedly knew him. They knew who he was, or rather, they *thought* they knew who he was. The common denominator with the people in your church and in your family is that they *think* they know who you are. In my case, they know that I struggle with my weight and that I am overweight. They know I have a mental illness and that I don't have a job apart from writing. They know that I am not confident in certain areas. They know my weaknesses.

They know the authentic you. They don't see you through the eyes of Jesus. They don't see your potential. They don't see the miracles that you can do. They don't believe that you can prophesy or that you can hear from God. They think they know you.

Because you are familiar to them, they won't recognize you as a prophet. They won't believe that you are special to God and that you are his close friend. They think they know you, and they think that they have a strong relationship with God and that you're just like they are. They don't think that you are special.

It's hard to convince them that you are a prophet. The Holy Spirit must speak to their spirit and convince them, and often they are closed to his voice. The Holy Spirit could tell them that you're a prophet, but they might think their mind is playing tricks on them. They won't believe the voice of the Holy Spirit.

It takes some time to be recognized as a prophet. At my last church, I was recognized as a prophet and was allowed to prophesy over anyone as I felt led. But the pastor didn't invite me to speak at church, although I've written many books, and I felt I was a gifted speaker. I left the church because of that. He was upset with me, and I told him that he should have invited me to speak. He replied, "You never asked to speak."

I thought it was poor protocol to ask a pastor, "Can I speak in church?" God puts it on the pastor's heart to invite you to speak. I was following proper protocol by not asking, but he insisted that if I had asked permission to speak, he would have let me speak. I was offended, and so I left. That probably wasn't the right thing to do. I've since made a point to re-establish this relationship.

A reader of one of my books who was impressed with my writing wanted me to meet his pastor. We had dinner with the pastor, and the pastor recognized me as a prophet and actually heard from God because he didn't know me. All he had to go on was the Holy Spirit. God told him I was a prophet, and he recognized me as such in that church. In this way, I found a new church.

Like I said, at the recent conference we had, he called me forth to speak a prophetic decree over Australia. He recognizes me as a prophet, and during the conference, he asked me for God's opinion and God's direction for the conference. He was seeking direction from me and accepting me in my prophetic office.

It can take quite a while for you to develop as a prophet in your church and for your local church to accept your calling as a prophet and believe that you're walking in the prophetic office. I've worked in the prophetic office for a number of years, and the church I currently attend recognizes that office in my life. The last time we had home fellowship, my pastor asked me to bring a message.

He is starting to ask me to speak and share and starting to use me in my giftings and my ability. It takes patience. Your family might never accept that you're a prophet. Like I've said before, Jesus says that a prophet will be honored everywhere else that he goes except in his own home and among his own family.

Do you expect your family, your home church, or the people you grew up with to recognize you as a prophet? Or do you accept that Jesus's words are true? Now that you know that Jesus's words were true for him in his own hometown and that he couldn't do miracles there like he could do everywhere else, does that give you hope?

I hope I've sufficiently answered your question. I feel for you. It's just a sad part of the prophetic life to be misunderstood and underappreciated by the people that should love us and respect us the most.

CHAPTER 8

How do I feel comfortable in my own skin as a prophet?

Life can be difficult as a prophet. As a prophet, you might feel like a fish out of water or like a square peg in a round hole.

It can be difficult to come to grips with the calling of a prophet. Normal people go to church and wear Jesus as a handbag, picking him up and taking him to church. They come home from church and put him down like a handbag and go on with the rest of their week without really thinking about Jesus.

As a prophet, you can't treat Jesus like that. He is with you every day, every hour, and every waking moment. You're aware of him and his love for you, and he's number one in your life.

How do you become comfortable in your own skin as a prophet? You have to learn what being a prophet is like. You have to learn who you're called to be as a prophet. Gaining an understanding of what a prophet is will take reading a lot of books. I've written five other books on the prophetic in addition to this one. This is my sixth book on the prophetic.

I'd recommend that you read all those books. I try and write books that are simple to understand and read, and I feel that I'm descriptive and helpful in what I've said about the prophetic and the prophetic office. I encourage you to read my other books.

As you read more and more books about the prophetic and about the life of a prophet, you will come to understand what you need to do as a prophet. The prophet's life is radically different from the life of most contemporary Christians.

You'll find out that prophets are radical, zealous, passionate, and on fire, and you'll learn that you really fit the mold of a prophet. You're not going to be comfortable in your own skin as a prophet until you find out what a prophet is truly like and how you tick.

You will understand more as you voraciously read books and listen to YouTube videos. Along with practicing your gift, these things will help you be comfortable in your own skin as a called prophet. You need to understand what a prophet is like and what the calling means and how to live as a prophet before you can actually come to grips with what you're called to be.

I suggest that you read books on the prophetic, books written by prophets, including Rick Joyner, Kris Vallotton, James Goll, Bill Hamon, Shawn Bolz, and others. You can read some books and research what a prophet is and how a prophet feels.

The more characteristics that you recognize in the life of a prophet, the more you come to grips with how prophets are radically different and strange individuals, the more you'll come to see those traits in yourself. You'll be able to transition into feeling comfortable with yourself and comfortable in your own skin as a prophet.

You might long to be like normal Christians and want to fit in with the typical Christian in church, but that simply won't happen for you. It simply isn't your reality, and you'll always have this struggle within yourself and within the Christian faith to assimilate with the normal Christians, which will be trouble.

I encourage you to a read my book, *Twenty-Two Signs that You're Called to Be a Prophet*. It's a very simple book and will help you recognize some of the characteristics of who you are and what you are like if you are called as a prophet.

I wrote the book for people to come to grips with their prophetic calling and recognize the twenty-two signs that accompany this call. You'll recognize many of those signs in your own life.

You will come to grips with that fact that indeed, you are called to be different. You are called to be radical. You are called to be passionate, zealous and on fire. The sooner you come to grips with those things, the sooner you can transition into living the life of a prophet.

CHAPTER 9

Is it normal to doubt my calling?

Part of the frustration of being called to be a prophet is coming to grips with the fact of your destiny. I think I had as many as twenty people prophesy over me that I was called as a prophet before I really came to grips with the fact of my calling.

It took twenty people—not one, not two, not three people—but twenty people to prophesy over me and confirm that I was called as a prophet before I accepted this. It's completely normal to doubt your calling.

I first felt called as a prophet when that apostle taught on the five-fold ministry. I figured out that out of all the offices, I was called as a prophet. I already realized my calling, but it took twenty people to prophesy to me before I quit doubting my calling.

The doubts can still manifest in my life, even after twenty years as a prophet. I still have reservations, worries, and fears that I'm not doing the right thing. I've come to grips with the fact that I am a prophet, a prophetic equipper, prophetic writer, and a prophetic evangelist.

When you are first starting out as a trainee prophet, the enemy will try to stir up doubt in you so that you question your calling. He'll try everything he can to divert you from the path of God in your life. Like anything worthwhile, the prophetic call takes persistence, perseverance, and patience. You don't start out with those qualities in your life.

You are on a journey to develop these characteristics. It takes life experience to develop those fruit in your life. You must travel along the road toward being a prophet for a number of years before you can completely fight off Satan's doubts in your mind.

Please expect that you'll have doubts. The reason that the Holy Spirit highlighted this question so that I used it as a chapter title was that doubting is an essential part of being a prophet. It's actually a building block. Doubts along the way are healthy because as you wrestle with these doubts, you'll find a sure footing and evidence through prophetic words and how God deals with you that will prove that you actually are a prophet.

In years to come, when people call you a false prophet and say that you're deceived and reject you publicly, your history with God will carry you. These former doubts and the evidence that God provided for you to be sure of your calling will hold you fast at times when you feel rejected and face trouble when you're actually walking in the office of prophet.

As you work through these early doubts about your calling, you will learn to hold firm in years to come when you're performing in the office of a prophet, waging warfare with the enemy. The enemy will bring opposition to you and your calling, and people will call you a false prophet, a heretic, and call you deceived, saying that you are preaching heresy.

These early assurances and confirmations will hold you steady when the boat starts to rock in the future. There is a plan and a purpose for these initial doubts. Follow the path before you and travel it proudly so that you can become the prophet that God has called you to be.

Don't feel bad about having doubts. They happen to everyone.

The twenty prophecies over my life and many subsequent ones along with many confirmations from God that I was called as prophet thrust me into a place where I actually became a prophet and could walk in my gifting.

I'm still not traveling, speaking, or ministering in churches internationally. I'm still not walking in the width and the breadth of my calling. I'm walking in the office of prophet, but I'm very hidden and not known by many people in the world. I don't have a big audience or platform. Nine hundred people—not ten thousand—read my books each month, but that's not as many people as read Joyce Meyer's books.

I'm relatively unknown at the moment, but I have no doubt that I'm in the office of prophet of God and no doubt of God's love for me. I have no doubt of my purpose in this world. God keeps on giving me things to do, books to read, blogs and books to write, things to say on Facebook, and YouTube videos to post. I can say that I have no doubt now. If you continue, you'll have no doubt in your life either.

CHAPTER 10

Is it common for prophets to want to quit?

I have to laugh at this one because it's such a tricky yet honest question. If you're honest with yourself as a prophet, you will admit that you've wanted to quit your calling so many times. In the early years, it's really hard, especially when you go through the refining fire or the wilderness experience. It's really hard to stay in the fight and fight as a good soldier, as Paul instructed Timothy in 2 Timothy 2:3–5. It's really hard to find the strength to go on through so much opposition—from demons, from the world, and from other Christians.

Someone will comment on one of your videos, teachings, or Facebook posts and call you a false prophet. You might try to argue with them that you're not a false prophet, and they are more eloquent with words. They might have hundreds and hundreds of scripture verses to quote back at you, which bother you. You might be convinced that you're not a prophet or even think that you're actually a false prophet because of what these people say.

These allegations from people that you're a false prophet might make you want to throw in the towel and say, "I quit. It's all too hard. They are probably right. I'm just fooling myself. I'm probably not a prophet and might even be leading people astray." Many people will come into your life, especially if you want to make an impact on others. They might attack you and say that you're a false prophet, a false teacher, and a heretic. You will face opposition. The enemy certainly doesn't want you to mature and become a true and authentic prophet who makes a lasting difference in people's lives. He will bring as much opposition to you as he possibly can.

This opposition will make you want to quit. Prophets are often uncomfortable with their calling and even resist it. A person who is comfortable as a prophet might need to re-evaluate themselves to see if they are really called.

Whether you are just starting out or you're an established prophet, it's understandable that you want to quit. These feelings are part of the life of a prophet. Deciding to quit and quitting for a week or a month or laying down your tools is common for a prophet. Like Peter said to Jesus after Jesus said to drink his blood and eat his flesh, "Where else can we go? You hold the words of life." (Paraphrase of John 6:68.)

You'll find that when you're called as a prophet, there's nowhere else you can go. You can't turn your back on God or on Jesus. You can't turn back to the world and start to drink or go back to other sin or run away like Jonah did. Sure, you can run from God for years, but God, in his mercy and his grace, will always have you return and bring you back to your calling. He will place a burden on your heart to make things right with him. So you can quit for a time, and God's grace allows that. He allows you to give up, and he will use many things—music, a sermon, a conference, a personal word from a friend or a stranger, or a YouTube video—to reignite the spark within you so that you turn back to him in repentance and start to pursue your prophetic calling again.

Don't be afraid if you're reading this book and you've tried to walk away from or deny your calling. Don't beat yourself up. If you are in a position where you want to quit, I have a lot of grace and understanding for you. I know what it's like to be in the fire, the refiner's fire. It can last for years. It can be very painful and tiresome, and you might just want to quit, walk away, and throw in the towel.

God knows your future. He knows why he created you. He has the ability to strengthen you. He has grace and the empowering work of the Holy Spirit to bring you to a place where you're comfortable, where you are

43

succeeding, where you are living as an overcomer. He enjoys you, and he loves you. Because he loves you, he'll allow you to have thoughts of quitting the race.

Once again, these thoughts of quitting are there to test you. They are stepping stones in your journey so that when tough times come in the future, when people are calling you a heretic and a false prophet, you won't quit your calling. When the real pressure starts, when the real stones are thrown, when you are in international ministry and people are calling you out as a false prophet, you will be reminded of your decision to persevere. You will be reminded of the earlier times when you wanted to quit and found a reason within yourself to stay the course. Those early days will give you the fortitude and the guts to stay the course in harsh times in the future. It's quite all right for you to want to quit. It's just a part of the prophet's life.

CHAPTER 11

Why did God choose me?

God calls people for a myriad of different reasons. Each individual is different; we all have different bodies, personalities, and backgrounds. We're different in every way, type, gender, leanings, and theologies. God calls so many of us because of that variety. He doesn't want people with the same personality and theology as prophets in the world.

He needs different prophets to impact different people. He needs prophets in every stream of the prophetic movement for all the different churches out there. He needs prophets who believe different doctrines and have different understandings to speak to people with those particular doctrines and understandings.

He usually needs people of the same race to speak to that race: a white person to speak to white people, black people to speak with black people, and Indian people to speak to Indian people. He needs all different cultures, shapes, sizes, and differences in people to speak to the different people that he's called us to.

He's an amazing God. You only have to look at creation and see the variety and the massive work that went into all of creation and all the birds, the bees, the flowers, and the different animals that make up this world to show you that God is a God of variety.

Because there is so much variety in the world, he needs a variety of people to minister to him and for him. Why did God choose you? He's a big God. He is smart and wise, and he knew that you could do the job, and he knew that you had the special characteristics in your background to make you a formidable prophet. He knew that you had resilience, perseverance, patience, and humility. He knew that he could fashion you into someone who could make a lasting difference in people's lives.

He chose you because you were unique. Everyone's unique, but he chose you because you had the guts and the fortitude to speak for him and represent him in the world. He knew that you'd have the courage and the resilience to fight a good fight and go on, despite your doubts, trials, and struggles, even when opposition came. He knew you would persevere and persist with your prophetic calling.

He chose you because you have a message that you need to release to the world. You have a burden on your heart that you want to share. You have answers for people with questions; you love those who feel unloved.

You have a desire to speak to people who are thirsty and hungry. You have sustenance when people are lacking; you have desire when many people have none. You have fire and passion when the world needs fire and passion. You have the answers that the world is looking for. You have so many attributes that God can use. He chose you even though you might not feel special, unique, or particularly gifted.

1 Corinthians 1:26–29 says,

For you see your calling, brethren, that not many wise according to the flesh, not many mighty, not many noble, are called. But God has chosen the foolish things of the world to put to shame the wise, and God has chosen the weak things of the world to put to shame the things which are mighty; and the base things of the world and the things which are despised God has chosen, and the things which are not, to bring to nothing the things that are, that no flesh should glory in His presence.

Paul said that God chose the foolish things of the world to confound the wise. God didn't choose the wise, the noble, the respectable, the good-looking, and the trained professionals to be his prophets. But he calls the foolish people of the world to make fools of the people who claim to be wise.

He's called you and me, who have no special ministry calling and no professional accreditation. He's called us to be his prophets and his spokespeople and friends, and as we minister to the people of God, we minister to him.

He loves you with an everlasting love. He desires that you serve him and minister for him and be his friend and keep him company on the dark and lonely nights that he has. He wants you to draw close to him and be his friend, someone he can count on to make changes in the world. These are some of the reasons that he chose you. I hope that ministers to your heart.

CHAPTER 12

How long do I have to go through the fire?

As long as it takes. An illustration about this follows. Someone asked a question of a refiner of precious metals. "How long do you have to refine the metal?"

And he answered, "As long as it takes."

They replied, "How do you set the heat?"

And he said, "I adjust the heat here."

They asked, "Well, how long do you refine it?"

He responded, "I refine it until I can see my reflection in it."

And so it is with you. You need to stay in the fire until Jesus can see his reflection in you.

Do you look like Jesus? Do you look like Jesus now, or do you have to work until you feel as if you represent Jesus? First John 2:6 says, "He who says he abides in Him ought himself also to walk just as He walked." The Apostle John lived without sin and preached that you can live without sin.

He was saying that if you say you have a close relationship with Jesus, you must walk like he did. Jesus didn't go around sinning, and he didn't have any faults. The Apostle John was saying that if you say you're walking with Jesus, you have to act like Jesus.

Are you acting like Jesus? Fire will continue until you are. The fire is brought into our life to burn away the dross, to burn away everything that's unclean, everything that is of no worth, everything that holds us back.

The fire will continue, and the refiner will adjust the heat and do exactly what God wants to do. God is a refiner, so he'll adjust the heat in our lives according to his purposes, according to what he wants to achieve.

You might know that I was addicted to prostitutes for many years. I entered counseling, and they taught me what true repentance was. I went to church and repented with all my heart one day, and my temptation to see prostitutes left me.

That week, I couldn't get out of bed at my normal time every morning. I'd go to bed at 10:00 p.m.; I couldn't get up until 5:00 p.m. the next day. I'd be up for a few hours, and then I'd want to go to sleep again. I found myself sleeping for twenty hours a day, which sent me into a very dark place, a really depressed state. The only way I could fight this sleep sickness, as I called it, was just to stay up for two or three days straight.

I kept myself busy by watching TV and writing Ezine articles to teach the Body of Christ. I'd stay up for two days and two nights, and then I'd go to sleep. I would then fall into the sleep sickness again and sleep from 10:00 p.m. until 5:00 p.m. the next day.

This went on for four years, and it seemed like it was my reward for giving up the life of addiction to prostitutes. I had a lot of pressure to go back to the prostitutes as I thought that might be a solution to stop my excessive sleeping. I was walking and talking with God after I'd been up for two or three days one time. I had a real connection with him. God told me that the sleep sickness was in my life to teach me endurance. A couple of my friends didn't believe that God had said that to me.

I was going to a counselor at the time, and I told the counselor and asked him if God really said that to me. He said, "Yeah, God did say that. You obviously don't know what endurance is."

I said, "No."

He said, "Endurance is the ability to continue against impossible odds." That's what was happening in my life. I was facing impossible odds. I can't explain how depressing it was to sleep twenty hours a day. I hardly had time to shave, clean myself, or wash my clothes. I was in a really bad place and was going through the fire with no end in sight. Instead of asking for the sickness to stop, my prayers turned to asking God to teach me endurance and to teach me my lesson well so that I could learn what he wanted me to learn.

Then one day, the sleep sickness stopped, and I was able to live a normal life. In the process, I'd written 850 Ezine articles, making a big impact. At one point, during the height of popularity for the articles, I'd reached 750,000 people. That's a lot of people! I learned to write, and years later, I started to write books.

As you can see from my personal testimony, the refining fire will last as long as it needs to last. God has a purpose and a reason for it. He wants to perfect you and strip away all your pride and your self-reliance. He wants to deal with all sorts of character flaws in you, and he'll continue to adjust the intensity of the fire until all those things are stripped away.

Is it normal to go through the wilderness? Why does this happen?

Sometimes the presence of God seems to leave you, and your ability to talk to God and to Jesus leaves. You enter a wilderness experience where you don't encounter God, and you can't hear from him.

This is a very scary place when you have an intimate relationship with God. One of the main reasons that God allows the wilderness to happen in a prophet's life is, once again, to strip away his compulsion for self-reliance and to remove any pride and character flaws.

It's a real refining process, and I found in my wilderness experiences that I was able to read the Bible and receive sustenance from the Word that I ordinarily wouldn't have. I found that because I wasn't hearing from Jesus and talking to him, I needed to hear from God. The only way I could hear from God was by reading the Bible.

He took me on a great journey of exploration of the Bible, and I came to a firm and thorough understanding of the scriptures through this experience. I probably haven't read the Bible as much as religion tells me I should have.

During that season, for years, I spent hours in the Bible, reading the Word of God and being encouraged by Isaiah. I have fond memories of this season.

Sometimes when you are sad, you can find a special comfort despite your sadness, and God can be especially close to you, even if you are depressed. This seems strange, but these are special and unique times. Even though I felt God was far away from me in this wilderness experience and I went through a number of these experiences, I know that God was as close as ever to me and was only a thought away. He was overshadowing me and carrying me on his wings, and I was just not aware of it.

The wilderness experiences happen to strengthen you so that you can be built up in the Bible and in other people's teachings. When you go through wilderness experiences as a prophet in training, I encourage you to dig deep into the Word of God and even buy a concordance and a commentary and read the Bible commentary. Dig deep into the Bible for an understanding of the Word. When you become busy in ministry, you might not have as much time to research or study the Bible in depth as you do in these wilderness seasons.

God does everything for a reason. He has purposes for everything he does, but the wilderness clearly is for your well-being so that you can learn to have confidence in God even when he doesn't seem to show up. Your faith is strengthened so that you can make it through and endure anything that comes against you. You will believe that God is a good God, and he only does what is right. Although you might not understand everything at the time or grasp why he's doing what he's doing, you need to wholeheartedly believe that he's loving, wise, and faithful.

When your faith is tested, it will be strengthened. If things are tested, they're real. You can have a whole lot of students who think they understand a certain subject. You can ask them if they understand the subject, and they can all be confident about how much they know. But it's not until you give them a test that you can see who truly understands the subject and who doesn't.

When our faith is tested through our wilderness experience, for instance, we really understand the level and the depth of our faith. When the times of testing come later in your prophetic life—when people are calling you a false prophet, a false teacher, or a heretic—what you learned in the wilderness and the faith that you developed during these times will hold you fast and give you the strength and endurance to hang on against all kinds of opposition.

CHAPTER 14

Will I ever be normal and fit in?

The answer to that question is simply no. You'll never be normal. You might have the grace to come to a church like I am attending at the moment where you do fit in, but even though people love and accept you, you might not speak at depth or at length on any of the subjects that are really burning in your heart. You can be loved and accepted to a point by people, but if you want to have a long conversation, you might not fit in.

It's only normal for us as humans to want to be loved and accepted and to fit in. No one wants to be the odd man out. No one wants to be a fish out of water. No one wants to be a square peg in a round hole. No one wants to be rejected and misunderstood, but this is the path of a prophet.

Part of the reason you're misunderstood, rejected, and you don't fit in is because God wants you to be *his* friend. He doesn't want you to rely as much on physical friends and friendships with people, but he wants you to be so close to him that he can trust you with his message and what he has called you to do. Most people in life feel normal and feel as if they fit in.

Yet you are called as a prophet, and you won't fit in or feel normal. Many Christians will hear about your supernatural life: meeting Jesus, meeting saints, having an open heaven over your life, working in the miraculous, and walking in a tremendous prophetic gifting. When they hear about your walk, they might be spiritually jealous of you and want that for themselves. This is both sad and hopeful.

A few of them might be prepared to pay the cost that it takes to have a life like that. A few of them have the strength, the ability, and the endurance to walk out that kind of life, but you can live that kind of life by being close and intimate friends with Jesus. If you were allowed to be normal and fit in, then you wouldn't develop such a close relationship with Jesus. Many of those who miss out on friendships and miss out on the love that they receive from others have a desire and a space in their heart to become close to Jesus.

People with friends and some close relationships might be able to grow close to Jesus, too, but you'll probably develop a deep and intimate relationship with Jesus when you have fewer friends and intimate relationships in the natural. You might not be normal or fit in.

If Moses and the people had been happy in Egypt, he could have never been used as the prophet who delivered the people from Egypt. If he were happy with what was going on in Egypt, he would have stayed in the palace and not caused any trouble and not killed anyone. He would have just lived his life in luxury, but he had to reach a place where he wasn't happy with the injustice coming against the Israelites so that God could actually use him.

Then he had his wilderness experience for forty years where he lived as a shepherd. God then called him to release the captives of Israel. So God has to call you, and you have to go through a wilderness experience. He has to put you through the fires to prepare you and consecrate your heart so that you are in a position to lead the people of God out of captivity and into the Promised Land.

You have to be unique because God wants the people of God to live, believe, and know differently. You have to understand the traits and the message of God, and you have to be able to bring that message to the people to bring them into the Promised Land that God has for them.

You can't be normal because if you're happy with a so-called normal life, you'll never have the answers for people. You'll never be able to show them a better or different way that will benefit them. But if you're different, if you don't fit in, then you'll be consecrated to the Lord. You'll be set apart for him and his purposes, and he'll be able to speak to you and teach and train you to have the information and the knowledge that can help people progress into a proper Christian life.

CHAPTER 15

Why am I so zealous and on fire when the church seems so dead?

That's a great question, and I'm glad you asked. As I said in the previous answer, if you're happy with a normal life, you can't be used to bring people to a new life. You have to be different: radical, zealous, and on fire so that you can bring a message to the dead church and bring them out of this slumber.

You have to have radical faith and a radical love for Jesus so that you can spread that consuming fire among people who are hungry. The church is dead and asleep, and someone has to wake them from their slumber.

I do that, book by book, one by one. I have some basic books for the average Christian on subjects like the parables of Jesus. These attract normal readers.

But I teach on radical subjects in some books when people want to read more books by me. I have more radical books. I wrote books on simple subjects to attract people. My books will take any person who starts to read them on a journey that becomes more and more radical.

I believe my books are waking up the church, waking up people and turning them from dead religion. They become more fired up and more zealous. That's just a little bit about me and my purpose, but I say it to illustrate the point that someone has to be on fire.

What's the easier way to start a fire: from scratch by putting two pieces of wood together and creating friction so that it smokes and catches fire or by using an ember and putting it on deadwood and seeing it spring up? This is a rhetorical question with an obvious answer: it's easier to use an ember. It's easier to light a dead church with a fiery ember. Someone has to be zealous and alive in order to bring that passion and that zeal to the Body of Christ.

As a prophet, you should be zealous and on fire. I write more about that in *Twenty-two Signs that You're Called to Be a Prophet*. If you have more questions about this subject, read that book because I go into much greater detail in it.

You have to realize that you are different; you're not normal. You're not a regular Christian. You're not a pew sitter. You're not just happy going to church on Sunday and saying one-way prayers to God. You have two-way conversations with God.

God not only speaks to you, but he leads you. He stokes the fire. The Holy Spirit and angels work with you to stir the fire of your heart. Your guardian angel actually fans the fire in your heart and keeps your fire burning. Your angel keeps you on fire and keeps you passionate, hungry, and thirsty for more of God.

Sometimes your angel just works nine to five to keep you hungry, searching, learning, and pressing forward.

What would you rather be? Would you rather be a random pew sitter, who is happy with how churches operate? Or would you rather be zealous and on fire and a bit frustrated with the church? Do you want to know the voice of God and know the answers that he has and the direction that he wants to take the church? Only an intimate son or daughter of God will actually know these things.

Those are interesting questions, and it's a shame that so much of the church is asleep and dead. I often wonder if people want revival because to revive means to bring someone back from the dead. When you say that you want revival, you're actually saying that the church is dead and needs to be revived. This is true for most of the churches in the world; they are dead and need reviving. The hungry, fire-filled passionate Christians like you will bring fire to that dead church and set it ablaze in revival. The church will never be the same again.

CHAPTER 16

Do ever reach a stage where you're comfortable that you know enough?

I have never reached a stage like that in my life, and I'm fifty-one years old now. I've been on this prophetic journey for twenty years. I've read many books and watched many YouTube videos. I'm always reading and learning, and I actually don't think that I know a lot about the prophetic.

I read books by people like Jeremiah Johnson, who is younger than I am. He seems so full of wisdom and knowledge, and he seems to know much more about the prophetic than I do. Here I am, writing my sixth book on the prophetic, and I'm sure that many of my readers think that I know so much more than they do.

I look at elders in the faith like Rick Joyner and Bill Hamon, who've been around the prophetic for forty to fifty years in ministry. I know that they know so much more than I do; they are so much more mature than I am. I know that I have so much to learn.

But I pass the information that I know onto other people in the simplest way possible so that I can equip other saints. I don't think I'll ever reach a place where I know everything, where I feel that I know enough. I think that's only wisdom on my part. I think it's also a sign of humility and the fact that I have a teachable spirit.

Someone who's teachable knows that you can always learn something new, and we all believe differently, so there's room for growth and room for us to change our beliefs and doctrines.

I know that people in heaven are always growing and learning and coming into new knowledge and moving from glory to glory. Even in heaven, I'll be growing and learning each week. I don't think you ever reach a point where you know enough.

Am I happy? I'm comfortable that I know enough to get by and that I can do the job that I'm called to do. I don't want to give you the impression that you have to pursue the prophetic for twenty years and not be comfortable with who you are. I'm comfortable with who I am. I'm comfortable with the knowledge that I already possess, but I'm hungry and thirsty and always seeking and pursuing more.

I enjoy learning and reading. I enjoy the Holy Spirit teaching me. I enjoy speaking to saints and receiving revelation from them. I enjoy my life. My life can be difficult, and it honestly *has* been difficult. I am comfortable with the books I've written, and the knowledge that I possess, and where I am.

I know so many people who are reading this book who would love to have the understanding of the prophetic that I have. They would love to have my wisdom. You might read things in this book that you wish you could understand. I'm sure that most of you understand what I've written in this book. So many of you will have come across information that you wished you could remember. You probably have to read this book more than once to absorb all the information in your spirit.

The difference between you and me is that I know this information. I haven't done research for this book. I only bought James Goll's e-book, *The Seer*, so that I could share the twelve different kinds of prophets. But besides that, I haven't done any research for this book. My life is my research.

This book is being recorded on twenty different voice files that are approximately nine minutes long. All the information for the book is coming from my spirit man. I know this information, and some of you readers, who are learning so much, really wish that you could know what I know.

The same is true for me when I read books by popular prophets. I'm in the same position; I need to read the books more than once, and I wish that I knew what that prophet knew. I realized that when you read any book, you only understand a portion of what the prophet actually knows and understands. I know prophets who know so much more than I do, and they have a lot more insight. I'm comfortable where I'm at, but I know that there's so much more to the prophetic and the kingdom of God.

CHAPTER 17

How do I deal with my loneliness?

That's a great question to ask, and I'm glad that you've asked it. I want to give you an empathetic answer to that question because I've been very lonely in my life.

I'm fortunate to have a mother who I can call a couple of times a day. I can talk with her about my life, and she's not burdened by my phone calls. I don't worry her too much as she has reassured me many times that she enjoys my phone calls and enjoys our friendship. I'm fortunate that I have someone to talk to.

I often talk with my friend, Mary Gibson, who I've mentioned in this book before. She's understanding and prophetic, and we have a lot to discuss. She's also read nearly every one of my books. I can talk to her about my books, and she understands much of what I understand and teach.

My close friend, Nicola, proofreads my books and also works on my prophetic website. She gives prophecies on my prophetic website. We talk almost every day, sometimes more than once a day. We have long phone calls. One phone call went for 4 hours, 44 minutes, and 44 seconds. If you're lonely and you like to talk and fellowship with people, then I'd imagine that you'd enjoy a phone call that long.

As I mentioned before, when you're lonely, you develop a close relationship with Jesus. Jesus seems to allow a lack of friends in your life to lead you toward himself so that he can become your source and become important in your life. When you have a close and intimate relationship with Jesus, he can start to trust you with friends so that you don't desert him and leave him behind.

I've lived with no friends for a number of years. I was entertained by the internet, books, and TV. I had a close relationship with Jesus. Like I mentioned, I spent a lot of time staying up and writing articles when I had the sleep sickness. It was interesting to write articles and see that people were blessed by what was written. I find that writing books and speaking to you, dear reader, brings me comfort.

I know that many of you have read this book and have been touched by it. Many of you who are reading are indeed lonely and want an answer to your loneliness. I feel that you could address this problem by writing, doing YouTube videos, and speaking, even if you're speaking to people who don't respond. Even if people don't like and comment on your Facebook posts or YouTube videos, you're still speaking. It removes a little bit of the loneliness in us. I've produced a book each month for two years now.

As I'm speaking to readers, I'm actually unburdening my heart. I'm really sharing my heart with the people of God, which is relieving my pain. It's healing some misunderstandings in my heart and helping me receive more clarity, understanding, and love for myself.

I find that speaking is very rewarding, and I'll pray for you, dear reader, that God would bring a person into your life to be a friend who can understand you and understand what makes you happy.

I pray that Jesus would provide you with one or two friends who you can speak to and share your life with and discuss revelations and what you're learning from God.

I can't speak to everyone. I don't have the time or the mental capacity to deal with speaking to an extra twenty people. If this book has impressed you, you could write to me and ask if we could chat over messenger or

Skype. Perhaps you just need a prophet as a friend to speak to once a week for half an hour to an hour. I can certainly invite you to connect with me. If you're in a position where you are really learning, and you just need someone to speak to, I encourage you to reach out to me because I have a little bit of time, and I can understand being lonely.

I suggest that you read. I suggest that you use your time to watch YouTube videos. I suggest that you find TV programs that you like. I suggest that you draw close to Jesus and that you read my book, *7 Keys to Intimacy with Jesus*. You can learn to speak to Jesus and learn to hear his voice.

You can also learn to hear Jesus speak through conversation and two-way prayer in my book, *How to Hear God Speak*. Find some interests. You can go to clubs or special interest groups. This is a really hard and difficult subject. Even if you follow all my suggestions, they might fall short. You might still be lonely at the end of the day. My prayer for you is that God will bring a friend into your life. If a friend doesn't appear in your life, certainly reach out to me at my Facebook address: https://www.facebook.com/matthew.r.payne

CHAPTER 18

Why do I always feel strange and the odd one out everywhere?

That is part of being a prophet. You're the odd one out. You're like a broken finger, pointing a different direction from all the other fingers. You're the ugly duckling. You're the one that got away; you're different; you're peculiar.

Peter calls us aliens, a peculiar generation, and those come from another world. (See 1 Peter 2:9–11.) You're unique and different.

As a prophet, you are not made to be the same as other people. When you are with others, they are often not speaking about subjects that really interest you. Many people discuss sports, entertainment, and TV shows, which you might not follow, so you can't participate in their mundane conversations.

Many Christians speak about fleshly things and things of the world. As a prophet, you're set apart and called out from the world. The things of the world don't impress you.

My former pastor and I watched some of the same shows and could have conversations about them. But most of the time, I like talking about Jesus and his revelations and what he's showing me. Very few people have the time to actually sit down and listen to what God is showing you. They might feel squeamish or uncomfortable listening to revelation that Jesus is giving you because Jesus doesn't speak to them, and they don't have revelation from him. They feel uncomfortable speaking to someone who says they do.

They don't always believe that Jesus is telling you things. Many people believe that you have a mental illness or have something wrong with you if you actually hear from Jesus. This might be true in some cases. I do have a mental illness. But most of the time, I do receive revelations, revelation from the Holy Spirit.

People are just uncomfortable with talking about Jesus and the kingdom all the time. Some Christians are passionate about the kingdom and all things God, and they are excited to talk about these subjects, but some of them aren't as committed as you are. Some of them are all talk and no action. They go from conference to conference and book to book; they are ever learning but never coming to an understanding of the truth. (See 2 Timothy 3:7.) Like Jesus said, they are pursuing information but never receiving that information. They are never practically demonstrating that knowledge.

In 1 John 2:6, we read, "He who says he abides in Him ought himself also to walk just as He walked." That means that you're not reading about Jesus and not thinking about Jesus, but you actually are being him. Transformation and change have happened in your life.

When you're acting and walking like Jesus, you just don't fit in with everyone. Everyone can love you to a point, but they only want to talk to you for five minutes. They don't want to sit down and speak for an hour and a half about what God is showing you.

People are so busy. They live such fleshly lives, lives full of sports, entertainment, and TV shows. They want to talk about their possessions, their jobs, and things of the flesh so often that you feel as if you're the odd one out. You feel like you're at the table, and people are talking, but you just don't fit in.

This is why God has called you to be separate to himself, because if you went and visited a galactic council in heaven, you would be happier. My book, *My Visits to the Galactic Council: Book 1,* will give you an idea of what I am speaking about. If you had a galactic council set up in heaven for you to visit, you could go up there all the time and talk all day with the saints, and you would have wonderful things to talk about, which would be a real pleasure and a great experience. I encourage you to read that book and visit the council to see the actual council members. I'm sure that they would welcome you to interact with them so that you could be friends. The fact of the matter is that you're wired differently than most of your friends, which is why you seem like the odd one out wherever you go.

CHAPTER 19

Will I ever teach and travel?

I've had so many prophecies over my life that say that I will travel the world, be an international speaker, and preach and teach to the Body of Christ. I've had many prophecies that say that I will run prophetic schools and equip people in the prophetic. At the moment, ministering in churches has not opened up to me, which I can understand because God is still preparing me. It's valid to wonder if you will ever preach and travel.

Many people only want to stay in their local setting and preach. I'd love to travel and teach people all over the place, speaking at conferences and at meetings in churches. We see so many people doing that.

As prophets, we have a message and a burden on our hearts to teach people. That's a natural desire, but it will only happen if God allows it and if he wants it to happen.

Sometimes we have to go through many years of training. As I mentioned earlier, I've been on my prophetic journey for more than twenty years. I'm still not preaching in other churches. I shared in my fellowship group last week, and in three weeks' time as I write this, I am scheduled to preach at church for the first time.

I just renewed my expired passport, so I'm ready to travel now. I just have to buy some nice clothes so that I am presentable. I've been losing weight, so I might have to buy clothes that are more flattering to me. I'm ready to travel when Jesus wants to open up that door to me.

If you've received prophecies that you will travel and teach, you can trust that in God's right time—when you've been refined, taught, and trained—you'll be released when God is ready to release you. But if your purpose is to be a hidden prophet at the moment, you can't do anything to open up doors for yourself.

If God wants you to remain hidden, you'll be hidden until the time when God wants to release you to start to preach. In the meantime, I stay happy by publishing a new book each month. Up to nine hundred people read my books each month. I feel that I'm already preaching. I'm going into people's households and teaching them, and I'm receiving a lot of feedback from people who have read my books. They are being encouraged, and so I feel that in some way, I'm touching people's lives.

If you're reading this, you might think that nine hundred people a month is amazing. You might think that's a lot of people. As I said before, I am comfortable with who I am and with what I know. I'm comfortable with what I'm teaching and what I possess, so I'm very happy.

Whether you will be able to preach and travel is completely up to the Lord. Sometimes the Lord just wants you to be a prophetic voice in your church and to preach in your church and impact the people that you do church with.

God has a different purpose for every prophet. I'm sure some prophets have never preached. They are intercessors who've prayed for the nations and affected countries with their prayers, but they've never had an active preaching itinerary like some other prophets.

Everyone seems to want to be in the pulpit, but no one wants to take the time to sit with God and be his friend. Many people want to stand before the crowds, but they don't want to wait before God and be his friend, someone that he can rely on.

I encourage you to take this time to get to know the Bible and get to know Jesus and be a true friend to him. Ask him to give you assignments for the kingdom and stay busy doing what Jesus gave to you to do and trust him. If you've received prophecies about speaking, teaching, and traveling, believe that it will happen in due time. Take time to relax and be patient with the Lord. Know that he is wise, and he is faithful. He will use you when he calls, when he feels the time is right to use you and not a day before.

CHAPTER 20

Am I worthwhile to the Body of Christ?

Many people watch international speakers or teachers speaking at conferences and on YouTube. But they don't feel worthwhile until they're on the stage and actually preaching. It's sad to think that your worth only comes when you're on stage. If you believe that, you will live without happiness, not fulfilling your purpose and not feeling worthy of even living.

In the meantime, you can do many things: write articles, create YouTube videos, post on Facebook, write books, and serve in many other ways. You can volunteer at a soup kitchen. You can learn to prophesy to people you know and to strangers.

You can walk around the soup kitchen and give people prophetic words and encourage them. You can learn to do prophetic evangelism and set up a table in your city with a sign that says, "Get your spiritual readings here." People will come to your table for prophecy, and you can prophesy over many people in a week.

You can do so many things and change so many lives with a prophetic gift. Over the course of many years, I've probably prophesied to over fifteen thousand strangers in my city. I have always given people an encouraging word. I have brought a corrective word to people on just a few occasions. Some prophets like to give corrective words to a lot of people, but that just doesn't seem to happen with my prophetic gift. I've been busy writing while I have been waiting to preach. I've written dozens of books, so many that I've lost count.

I feel that I'm very worthwhile to the Body of Christ. So are you if you have a prophetic gift, if you have the gift of prophecy. Ask the Lord each day to give you an opportunity to use your prophetic gift on someone.

I wrote a book called *Prophetic Evangelism Made Simple*, which you can order to learn how to prophesy to strangers. I explained how to do this quite simply in that book, and you can make a difference in one or two people's lives with a prophetic word as you go into the marketplace and mix with people.

I encourage you to write and make YouTube videos. I encourage you to make a difference. Use the skills and talents that God has given you to make an impact in your world.

The world is waiting for you. The world was created for you to take possession of it. You've been created for a purpose. You read this book for a reason. Jesus wanted me to speak to you and encourage you with the following:

- You are worthwhile.
- You are precious.
- God has called you as a prophet.
- He will use you to do great things, and
- Great things can actually be just leading one person to the Lord or prophesying over one person a week.

Great things don't have to be healing the sick or raising the dead. You can just transform one person's life with a prophecy, which can be a great thing. God can use you to do many things and influence many people. As a prophet, you are worthwhile to the Body of Christ, and God needs messengers.

He needs people to go out and influence the church. He needs people to speak on his behalf. Many in the Christian church can't hear from God.

You can speak to so many people who are waiting to hear from God if you have a prophetic gift. So many people desperately want to hear from him. You can help them if you are clearly hearing from God and if you practice hearing from him for others. You can join prophetic groups on Facebook and offer to prophesy over people. You can be busy prophesying over people and practice sharpening your gift.

You can do so many things if you change your attitude and adopt a positive mindset and become happy about what you are called to be.

I pray that this book has encouraged and blessed you. I hope that you had many of your questions answered. I know that the Holy Spirit and my scribe angel gave me the actual questions to address. They both allowed me to speak and gave me the right words to say. As Lisa Thompson, my editor, goes through my words and refines and polishes them, this book will be great. By the time you read this sentence, every sentence in the book will have been edited and thoroughly checked and perfected. You will have the best product that I could possibly have produced.

Let me pray for you now.

Dear Jesus, I pray that a fresh impartation of my anointing will flow onto you and that the Lord would fill you with his presence each day and walk with you. I pray for an open heaven over your life so that you might hear from Jesus. I pray that you will see Jesus in visions and have visitations from saints. I pray that you will visit heaven. I pray that your prophetic gift would increase. I pray for favor in your life. I pray that my mantle would start to rest on some of you prophets. I pray that you would be inspired to teach and to reach people and to encourage them. I pray that you would come to grips with the fact that you are very worthwhile to the people of God. In Jesus's name, I ask these things.

Be blessed.

I'd love to hear from you

One of the ways that you can bless me as a writer is by writing an honest and candid review of my book. I always read the reviews of my books, and I would love to hear what you have to say about this one.

Before I buy a book, I read the reviews first. You can make an informed decision about a book when you have read enough honest reviews from readers. One way to help me sell this book and to give me positive feedback is by writing a review for me. It doesn't cost you a thing but helps me and the future readers of this book enormously.

To read my blog, request a life-coaching session, request your own personal prophecy, or receive a personal message from your angel, you can also visit my website at http://personal-prophecy-today.com All of the funds raised through my ministry website will go toward the books that I write and self-publish.

To write to me about this book or to share any other thoughts, please feel free to contact me at my personal email address at

survivors.sanctuary@gmail.com

You can also friend request me on Facebook at Matthew Robert Payne. Please send me a message if we have no friends in common as a lot of scammers now send me friend requests. I am starting a community church meeting on zoom and training people in the prophetic over the zoom platform, so make sure you get in touch to be part of that.

You can also do me a huge favor and share this book on Facebook as a recommended book to read. This will help me and other readers.

How to Sponsor a Book Project

If you have been blessed by this book, you might consider sponsoring a book for me. It normally costs me between fifteen hundred and two thousand dollars or more to produce each book that I write, depending on the length of the book.

If you seek the Holy Spirit about financing a book for me, I know that the Lord would be eternally grateful to you. Consider how much this book has blessed you and then think of hundreds or even thousands of people who would be blessed by a book of mine. As you are probably aware, the vast majority of my e-books cost ninety-nine cents, which proves to you that book writing is indeed a ministry for me and not a money-making venture. I would be very happy if you supported me in this.

If you have any questions for me or if you want to know what projects I am currently working on that your money might finance, you can write to me at survivors.sanctuary@gmail.com and ask me for more information. I would be pleased to give you more details about my projects.

You can sow any amount to my ministry by simply sending me money via the PayPal link at this address: http://personal-prophecy-today.com/support-my-ministry

You can be sure that your support, no matter the amount, will be used for the publishing of helpful Christian books for people to read.

Other books on the prophetic by Matthew Robert Payne

- *The Prophetic Supernatural Experience*

- *Prophetic Evangelism Made Simple*

- *A Beginner's Guide to the Prophetic*

- *Deep Calls unto Deep: Answering Questions on the Prophetic*

- *Twenty-Two Signs that You're Called to Be a Prophet*

Upcoming books:

- *Michael Jackson Speaks from Heaven, Book 2: A Divine Revelation*

with Nicola Whitehall

- *Jesus and Mary Speak from Heaven: A Divine Revelation*

Acknowledgments

Jesus:

I want to thank you for being my lifelong friend and for never deserting me, no matter how dark my life became. You led me into some great adventures, such as writing this book.

Holy Spirit:

I want to thank you for leading and teaching me. You are a great teacher, better than I could ever be. You have been with me every step of the way. Thank you for your help with this book.

Father:

Thank you for loving me and entrusting me with this life that I am living. Thank you for revealing my purpose to me and leading me toward accomplishing it. Thank you so much for your Son, Jesus. Thank you for everything that you have done in my life. Thank you for leading me to help more people with another book.

Lisa Thompson:

I want to give special thanks to Lisa for editing this book of mine. You take my simple words and transform them to make me seem smarter than I really am. If you have any editing needs, you can contact Lisa at writebylisa@gmail.com

Nicola:

I want to thank Nicola for being part of my team as a proofreader. I want to thank you for all the work that you did with this book to polish and improve it. I love every phone call I have with you.

Friends:

I want to thank Darla, Lisa, Nicola, Mary, Wendy, Laura, David Joseph, and Michael Van Vlymen for your friendship and for how you have impacted my life.

Mom and Dad:

I want to thank my mother and father for all the love that they have given me. I am a product of your love.

Readers and ministry supporters:

I want to thank the readers of my books and my ministry supporters for the funds that you have given me to publish books. I live to educate people, and I thank my readers and the supporters of my ministry because you make life worth living.

About Matthew Robert Payne

Matthew Robert Payne, a teacher and prophet, enjoys writing what the Lord puts on his heart to share. He receives great pleasure from interacting with others on Facebook, hearing from people who have read his books, and prophesying over people's lives. He is a passionate lover and disciple of Jesus Christ. He hopes that as you discover his books, you will intimately come to know Jesus, the Father, and Matthew himself though his transparent writing style.

Matthew grew up in a traditional Baptist church and gave his heart to Jesus Christ at the tender age of eight years old. That changed when he left home at the age of eighteen. He lived a wild life for many years, engaging in bad habits and addictions. At twenty-seven, he was baptized in water and, at the same time, baptized in the Holy Spirit. Matthew learned about the five-fold ministry offices and received a revelation of their value today.

He started his journey as a prophet twenty years ago, learning about this gift and putting it into practice. With thousands of prophecies under his belt, he can confidently prophesy to friends and strangers alike. He has been writing for a number of years and self-published his first book in

2011. Today he spends his time earning money to self-publish and writes a new book approximately every month.

You can connect with him on Facebook. You can sow into his book-writing ministry, read his blog, receive a message from your angel, or even receive your own nine-minute personal prophecy from Matthew at http://personal-prophecy-today.com

Blurb

Prophetic gifts and the office of a prophet might seem confusing to you. You might wonder if you are called to this office, how to know if you're called, what the call entails, and how to walk out your calling.

Matthew Robert Payne has operated in prophetic giftings and walked in the office of a prophet for two decades. In his sixth book on this fascinating subject, he addresses the following:

- The function and role of a prophet
- Depression, rejection, and loneliness in prophets
- Walking through the wilderness and the fire as a prophet
- Learning how to walk in the prophetic anointing
- The value of a prophet to the Body of Christ and much more.

This informational book comes packed with great insights from a seasoned prophet who has walked through many difficult experiences. Matthew handles your tough questions with helpful and practical answers.